GREEK MYTHOLOGY

# APHRODITE,

## Goddess of Love

BY JOANNA BLAIR

Enslow PUBLISHING

**Please visit our website, www.enslow.com. For a free color catalog of all our high-quality books, call toll free 1-800-398-2504 or fax 1-877-980-4454.**

**Cataloging-in-Publication Data**
Names: Blair, Joanna.
Title: Aphrodite, goddess of love / Joanna Blair.
Description: Buffalo, NY : Enslow Publishing, 2027. | Series: Greek mythology | Includes glossary and index.
Identifiers: ISBN 9781978550773 (pbk.) | ISBN 9781978550780 (library bound) | ISBN 9781978550797 (ebook)
Subjects: LCSH: Aphrodite (Greek deity)--Juvenile literature. | Goddesses, Greek--Juvenile literature. | Mythology, Greek--Juvenile literature.
Classification: LCC BL820.V5 B535 2027 | DDC 292.2114--dc23

Published in 2027 by
Enslow Publishing
2544 Clinton Street
Buffalo, NY 14224



Portions of this work were originally authored by Christine Ha and published as *Aphrodite*. All new material in this edition was authored by Joanna Blair.

Cover Designer: Joshua Olson
Interior Designer: Joshua Olson
Editor: Claire Vanden Branden

Photo Credits: Cover, pp. 1, 14–15, 22–23, 29 Zwiebackesser/Shutterstock.com; pp. 4–5 Leni Kovaleva/Shutterstock.com; p. 6 Lev Levin/Shutterstock.com; pp. 6–7 f8grapher/Shutterstock.com; pp. 8–9 Gianluca Rasile/Shutterstock.com; pp. 10–11 Achim Wagner/Shutterstock.com; pp. 12–13 Shiler/Shutterstock.com; pp. 16–17 Myroslava Bozhko/Shutterstock.com; p. 18 Dimitrios P./Shutterstock.com; p. 19 Marinodenisenko/Shutterstock.com; pp. 20–21 Pupanjan/Shutterstock.com; p. 24 Moreno Soppelsa/Shutterstock.com; p. 25 Yusuf Tatliturk/Shutterstock.com; pp. 26–27 Yasemin Ozdemir/Shutterstock.com.



Printed in China

CPSIA compliance information: Batch #QS27ENS: For further information contact Enslow Publishing, at 1-800-398-2504.

# TABLE OF CONTENTS

4

CHAPTER 1

# GREEK GODDESS

Aphrodite was the Greek goddess of love. She was the goddess of beauty, too. She was very pretty.

**The Romans had their own versions of Greek gods. The Roman goddess of love was called Venus.**

Legends say Aphrodite was born near the island of Cyprus. But she was never a baby. Instead, she rose up out of the ocean. Then she floated to shore.

**Ruins of a temple for Aphrodite still stand in Cyprus.**

Cyprus is an island country in the Mediterranean Sea.

Some people said Aphrodite **protected** sailors.

In one legend, Aphrodite's tears created red flowers when a person she loved died.

Aphrodite could make people fall in and out of love. She fell in love, too. She loved both gods and humans.

## A MAGIC BELT

**Aphrodite wore a type of belt called a girdle. It had magical powers. Humans and gods would fall in love with whoever was wearing it.**

# CHAPTER 2

# FAMOUS MYTHS

The Greeks told many **myths** about Aphrodite. One said she married Hephaestus. He was the god of fire and metalworking. In another, she fell in love with Ares. He was the god of war.

**In art from ancient Greece, Ares was often shown as an armed warrior.**

Aphrodite gave Hippomenes golden apples to distract Atalanta during their race.

In one story, Aphrodite helped a man named Hippomenes. He wanted to marry Atalanta. But she would only marry someone who could beat her in a race. Hippomenes asked Aphrodite for help. The goddess helped him win.

## A MAN AND A STATUE

One story tells of a **sculptor** who fell in love with his statue. Aphrodite was moved by his love. She brought the statue to life.

The goddess Aphrodite had great power.

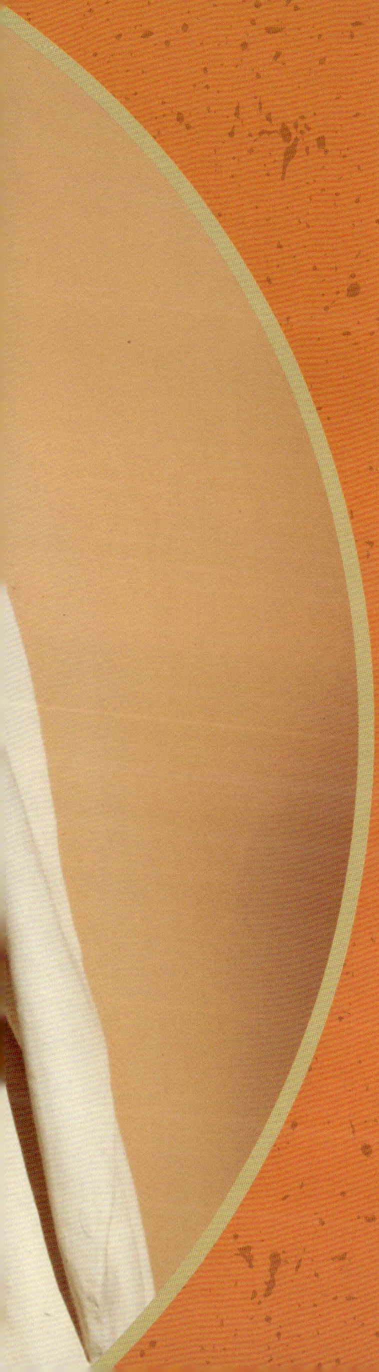

Another myth told of a woman named Psyche. She was so beautiful that people stopped loving Aphrodite. Aphrodite became jealous. She put a **curse** on Psyche.

**Aphrodite was known for her short temper. She would cause harm to people who made her angry.**

# CHAPTER 3

# PARIS'S CHOICE

**O**nce, three goddesses fought over who was most beautiful. A man named Paris was asked to decide. But each goddess tried to **bribe** him.

**Paris and Helen were two people that Aphrodite brought together.**

**Athena was the Greek goddess of war and wisdom.**

Athena promised to help Paris win wars. Hera said she would make him a ruler. Aphrodite said the most beautiful woman in the world would be his wife.

**The most beautiful woman's name was Helen. Her husband was the king of Sparta.**

**Aphrodite sometimes punished people. She made Narcissus fall in love with his reflection.**

Eros is better known by his Roman name, Cupid. He is often shown with wings.

Paris picked Aphrodite. She made Helen fall in love with Paris. Helen was already married. But she left with Paris. Their actions started a war.

## MAGIC ARROWS

**Eros often teamed up with Aphrodite. He shot two types of arrows. One kind made people fall in love. The other kind stopped people from falling in love.**

CHAPTER 4

# LOVE AND HONOR

Aphrodite was a **popular** goddess. People prayed to her for help with love and marriage. She could even change how people looked.

**In some cities, people honored Aphrodite as a war goddess.**

Aphrodite's main places of **worship** were in Cyprus. But she had followers all over Greece. She also had temples in the surrounding areas.

**The main entrance to one of Aphrodite's temples still stands in Turkey.**

Several cities were dedicated to the goddess Aphrodite.

# A BIG FESTIVAL

The people of Cyprus held a **festival** each year. It honored Aphrodite. The festival took place in spring. It lasted several days.

Stories of Aphrodite have inspired many famous works of art.

Shells and mirrors were important to Aphrodite. So were swans. People brought these things to her temples. They also offered **incense** and flowers.

**In some stories, Aphrodite rode a golden chariot. A team of doves pulled it.**

# TEST YOUR KNOWLEDGE

*Take this quiz to test your knowledge.*

1. Write a few sentences explaining the main ideas of Chapter 4.
2. Do you think it would be more helpful to make people fall in love or out of love? Why?
3. Which goddess did Paris choose as the most beautiful?
   A. Aphrodite
   B. Athena
   C. Hera
4. Why might shells be a symbol of Aphrodite?
   A. Shells come from the ocean, where she was born.
   B. Shells come from animals, which she ruled.
   C. Shells can hold pearls, which she wore.

5. What does **followers** mean in this book?

*Aphrodite's main places of worship were in Cyprus. But she had **followers** all over Greece.*

A. people who get lost
B. people who believe in a god or goddess
C. people who cook food

6. What does **offered** mean in this book?

*People brought these things to her temples. They also **offered** incense and flowers.*

A. gave something to a goddess
B. sold something at a store
C. lost something at sea

*Answers can be found on page 32.*

# GLOSSARY

**bribe**
To give someone gifts or money to sway a choice or action.

**chariot**
A two-wheeled cart pulled by horses or other animals.

**curse**
Something that brings harm or suffering.

**festival**
A day or time of celebration, often based on a religion.

**incense**
A spice that is burned to make a sweet smell.

**myths**
Well-known stories from the past that often include magic.

**popular**
Liked by or known to many people.

**protected**
Watched over or kept safe.

**sculptor**
A person who carves art from stone, wood, or other hard materials.

**worship**
The ways people honor or pray to a god or goddess.

# FOR MORE INFORMATION

## BOOKS

Curtis, Kenny and Jillian Hughes. *Greeking Out: Epic Retellings of Classic Greek Myths*. Washington, DC: National Geographic, 2023.

Ward, Marchella. *Gods of the Ancient World: A Kids' Guide to Ancient Mythologies*. New York, NY: DK Publishing, 2023.

## WEBSITES

**Britannica Kids: Aphrodite**
*kids.britannica.com/kids/article/Aphrodite/352766*
Read more myths about Aphrodite at this website.

**National Geographic Kids: The Gods and Goddesses of Ancient Greece!**
*natgeokids.com/nz/discover/history/greece/greek-gods*
Learn more about Greek gods and goddesses.

**Publisher's note to educators and parents:** Our editors have carefully reviewed these websites to ensure that they are suitable for students. Many websites change frequently, however, and we cannot guarantee that a site's future contents will continue to meet our high standards of quality and educational value. Be advised that students should be closely supervised whenever they access the internet.

# INDEX



**Answer Key:**
1. Answers will vary; 2. Answers will vary; 3. A; 4. A; 5. B; 6. A